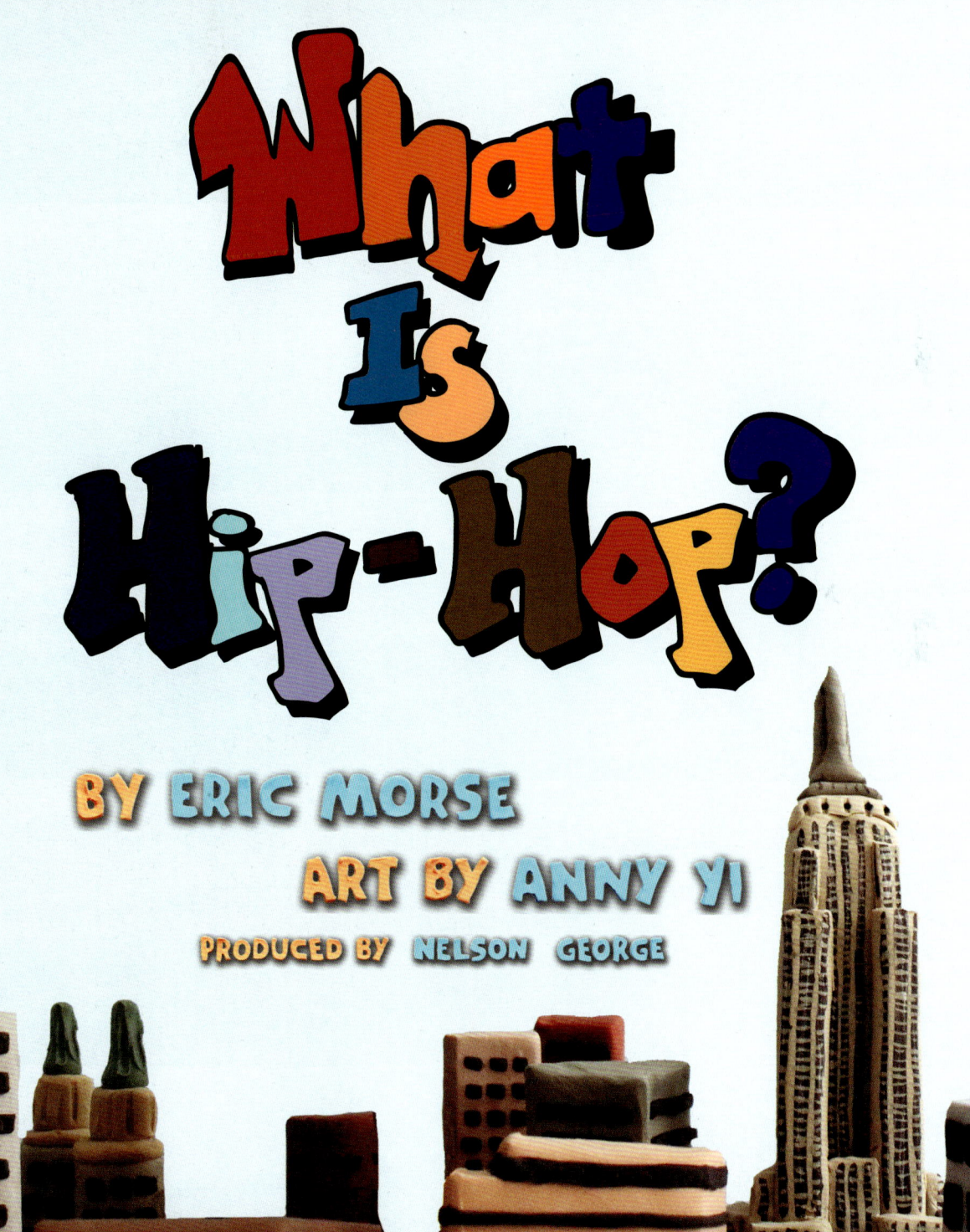

What Is Hip-Hop?

BY ERIC MORSE

ART BY ANNY YI

PRODUCED BY NELSON GEORGE

Words ©2017 Eric Morse
Illustrations ©2017 Anny Yi

ISBN: 978-1-61775-584-2
Library of Congress Control Number: 2017935216
Second printing

Printed in China

Black Sheep
c/o Akashic Books
Brooklyn, New York
Instagram, Twitter, Facebook:
AkashicBooks
info@akashicbooks.com
www.akashicbooks.com

AY: For DSY and JY

EM: For Eli, Owen, Eleanor, and Darby. And for Mom and Dad,
who didn't get it but supported my love for it.

In the beginning,
there was a beat.
Two records spinning,
and the crowd got on its feet.

B-boys and B-girls
started getting down,
and soon the whole world
was in love with the sound.

They called it hip-hop!
A whole new mystique.
Not disco or pop,
it was totally unique.

The Boogie Down Bronx is where our story begins.
That's where DJ KOOL HERC made the records spin.

Herc put the same track on tables one and two,
and bounced the beat back to make something new.

And Grandmaster Flash, a DJ one-man band,
revolutionized the scratch with his lightning-fast hands.

When you're close to the edge, it's a struggle to survive.
That's the story of "The Message," by Flash and the Furious Five.

Boogie Down Productions had a political flow—
KRS-One and Scott La Rock sure could put on a show!

The world lost Scott way before his time,
But KRS went on to preach UNITY.

If I ruled the world, all the boys and girls would know
the man who brought us all "The Breaks": the one & only Kurtis Blow.
He came from Harlem, the first rapper to go gold.
"The Breaks" broke a record with half a million sold!

Kurtis had another song that was bigger than them all.
An ode to his favorite sport: we're talking "Basketball."

Then a muscular teen from the borough of Queens,
in a Kangol hat,
burst on the scene.

He went by the name Ladies Love Cool James,
and in no time flat
earned his worldwide fame.

He was known as LL, he was rocking the bells.
When he stepped up to bat,
he was doing it well.

LL Cool J loved girls around the way;
don't call it a comeback,
'cause he was here to stay.

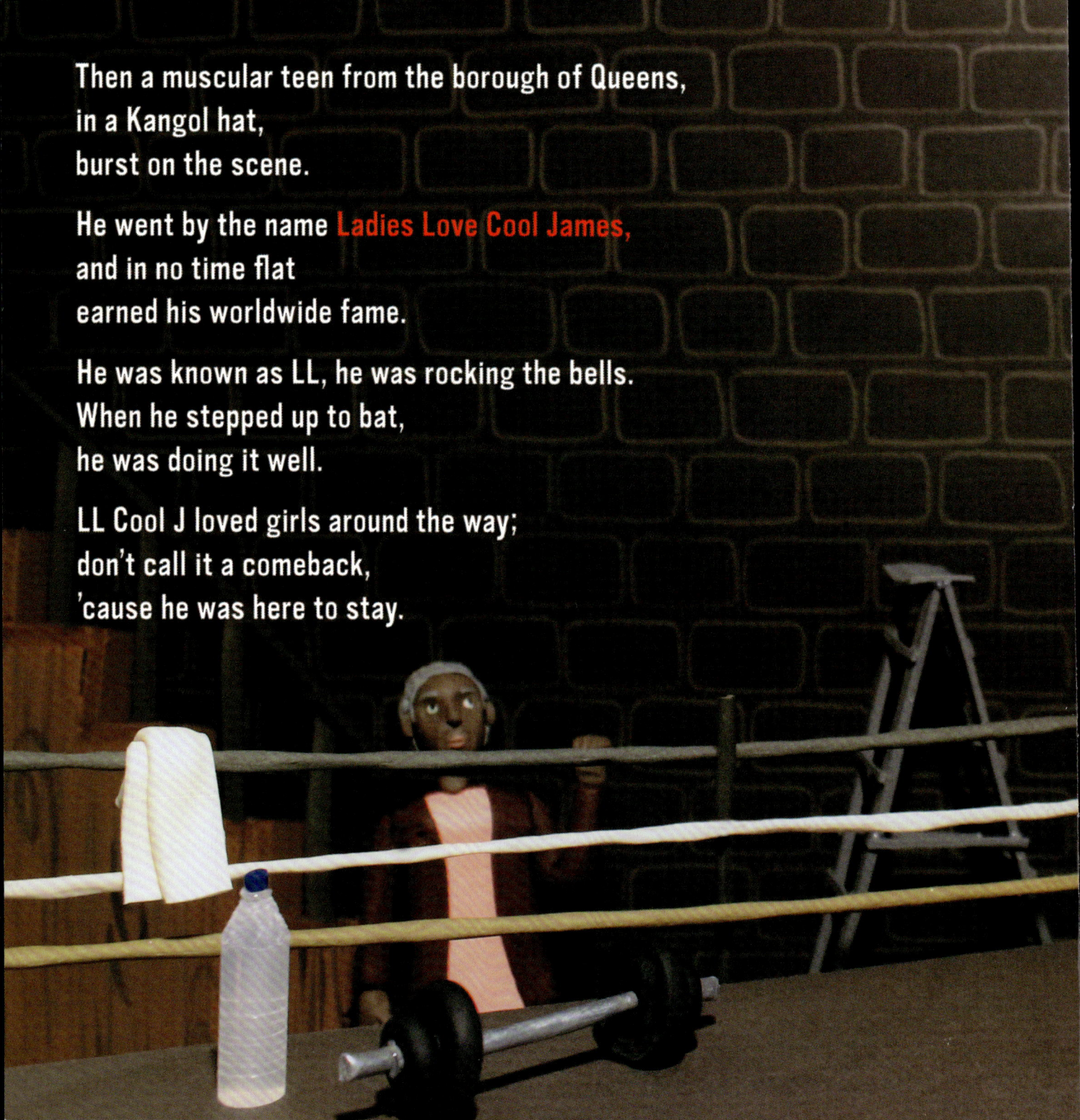

While we're on the subject, let's get another thing clear: there's much more to hip-hop than what you can hear!

B-boys and B-girls gave the world something new; graffiti and break-dancing defined hip-hop too.

Graffiti kids made murals where people could see 'em.
Brick walls and subway cars were their urban museum.

All the break-dancers rock their bodies to the beat;
don't need anything fancy—just cardboard in the street.
Popping, locking, and a whole lot more—
the windmill and the worm and backspins on the floor.

Joe plus Darryl equals **RUN-DMC**.
Add Jam Master Jay and the pair makes three.

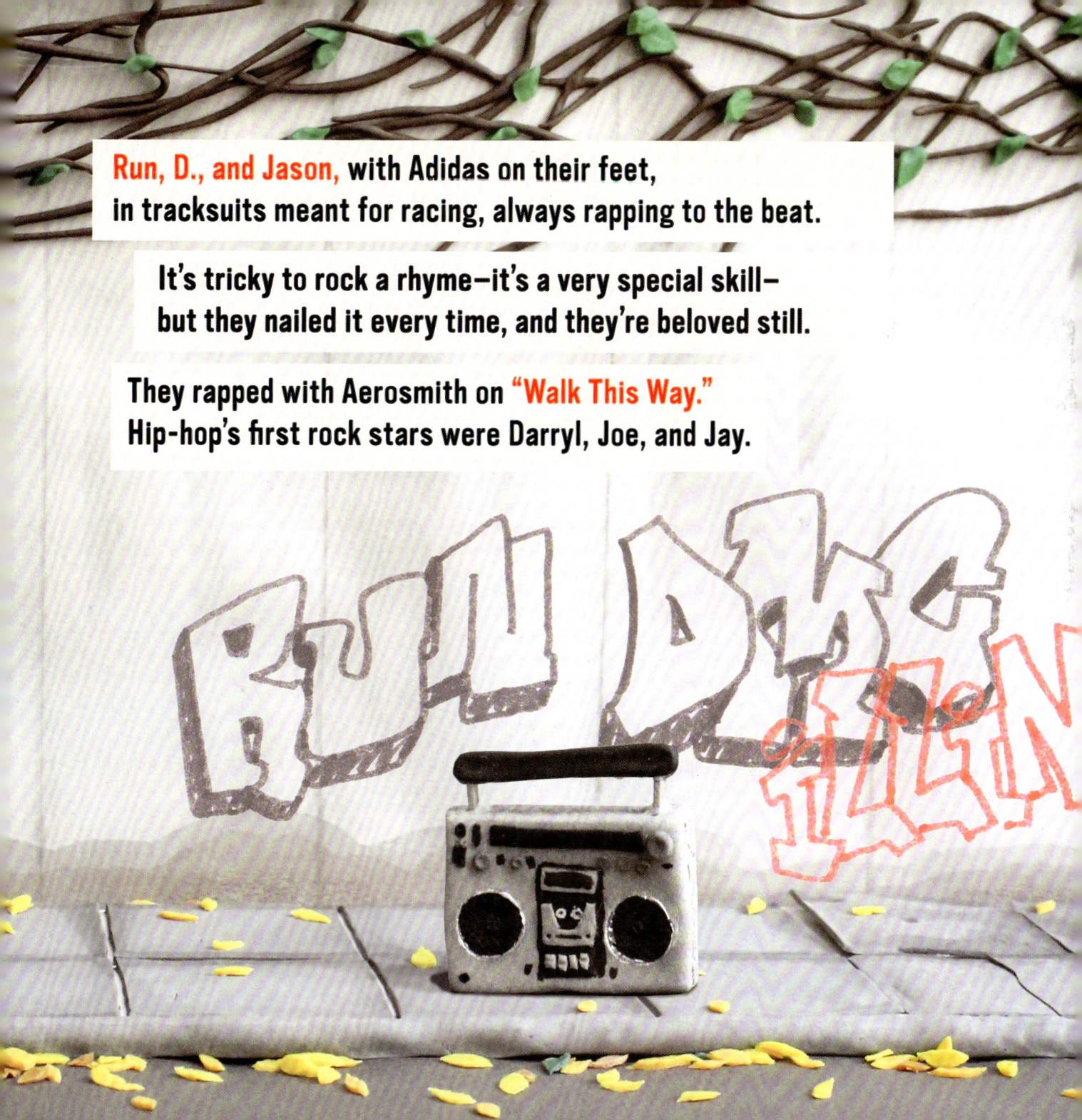

Run, D., and Jason, with Adidas on their feet,
in tracksuits meant for racing, always rapping to the beat.

It's tricky to rock a rhyme—it's a very special skill—
but they nailed it every time, and they're beloved still.

They rapped with Aerosmith on **"Walk This Way."**
Hip-hop's first rock stars were Darryl, Joe, and Jay.

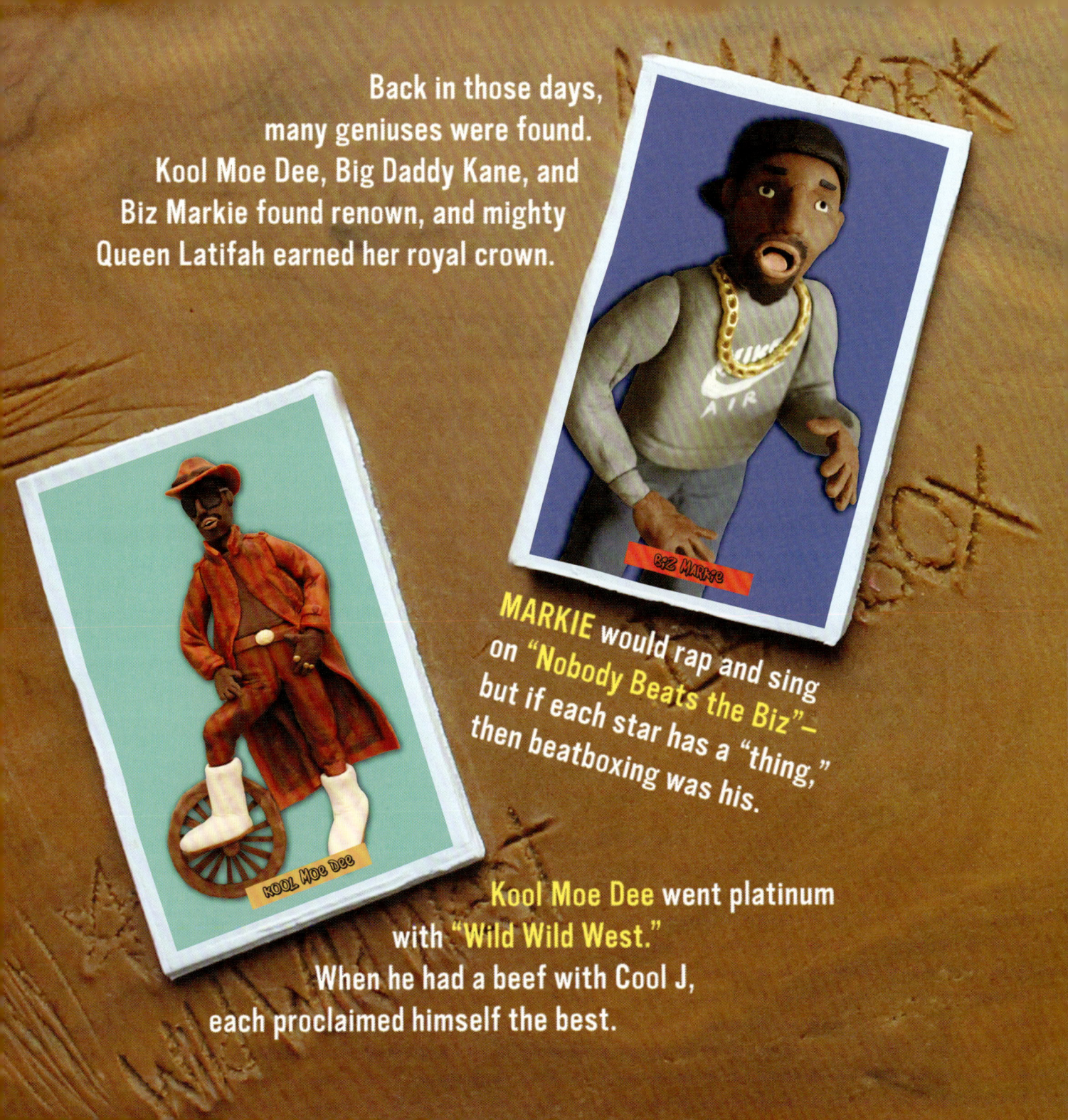

Back in those days,
many geniuses were found.
Kool Moe Dee, Big Daddy Kane, and
Biz Markie found renown, and mighty
Queen Latifah earned her royal crown.

BIZ MARKIE

KOOL MOE DEE

MARKIE would rap and sing
on "Nobody Beats the Biz"—
but if each star has a "thing,"
then beatboxing was his.

Kool Moe Dee went platinum
with "Wild Wild West."
When he had a beef with Cool J,
each proclaimed himself the best.

Big Daddy Kane had skills
like no one ever saw.
MCs all made way
whenever Kane got raw.

QUEEN LATIFAH
stood out too
as one of the best
to ever do it.
She'd go toe to toe
with anyone,
and every rapper
knew it!

QUEEN LATIFAH

BIG DADDY KANE

Rakim's the microphone fiend and Eric B. is president;
the lyrics were esteemed, DJ skill was evident.

The words could paint a picture with syncopated rhyme.
A magical hip-hop mixture, among the best of all time.

Hip-hop loves a party, and EVery PARty NEEDS a **BEAT.**
But sometimes you gotta fight the POWER and take it to the streets.
CHUCK D and **FLAVOR FLAV,** a legendary pair,
shined a light on racism and a world that was unfair.

B-E-A-S-T-I-E
I'll spell the word out, so everyone can see
Ad-Rock, MCA, and Mr. Mike D,
fighting for their rights most definitely.

They had a funny way with words, and they loved '70s funk.
They could sometimes be heard playing good old-fashioned punk.

The world was astounded when they dropped *Paul's Boutique,*
at the fresh way it sounded and the sampling technique.

Three was the magic number
for these plugs from Long Island,
who first made their name
with *3 Feet High and Rising.*

People called them hippies, with their hair up in dreads,
but De La Soul had talent and earned their hip-hop cred.

Plugs 1, 2, and 3
climbed to the top.
De La Soul blew up,
but they never went

POP!

DE LA SOUL

Two talented ladies
in a field full of boys,
Salt-N-Pepa held their own
and played them all like toys.

Rap royalty from Queens, no pun intended,
their songs weren't always clean,
some people were offended.

But "Push It" was the jam;
so was "Whatta Man."
Their success was proof
girls can do what boys can.

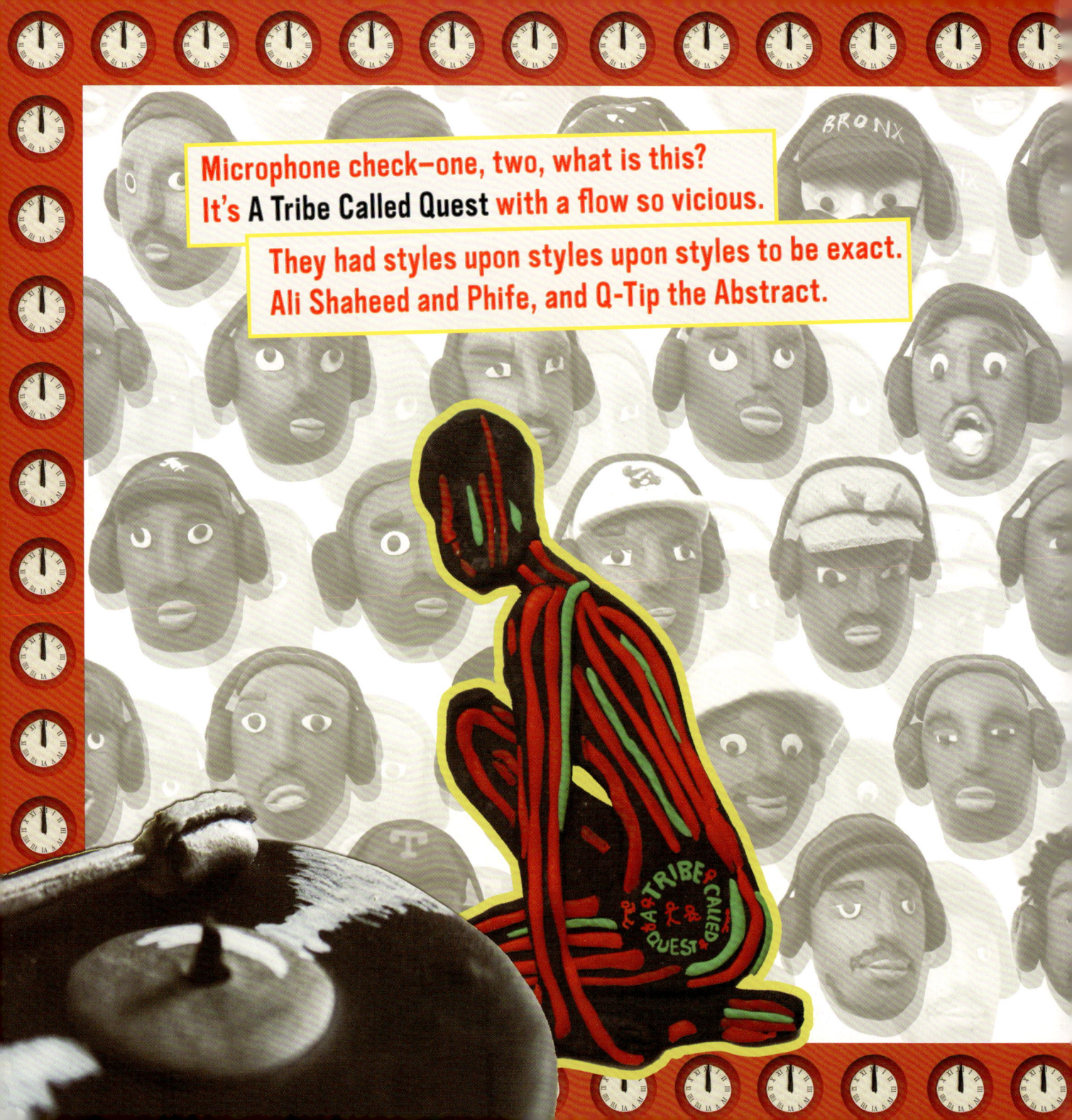

Microphone check—one, two, what is this?
It's **A Tribe Called Quest** with a flow so vicious.

They had styles upon styles upon styles to be exact.
Ali Shaheed and Phife, and Q-Tip the Abstract.

Midnight Marauders and **Beats, Rhymes and Life** made hip-hop heroes out of Ali, Tip, and Phife.

4 MCs and 1 DJ straight outta Compton in South Central LA—
Yella, Ice Cube, and Eazy, MC Ren, and of course Dr. Dre.
Put them all together and you get **N.W.A.**

There was violence in their songs,
and other bad things too.
Call it right or call it wrong,
they sang of the world they knew.

One rapper stood out
from the others pictured here.
Ice Cube was about to have a storied career.

Cube was no lazy slacker—
he became an all-time great.
As a rapper and an actor, he knew how to captivate.

Bow wow wow, yippee-yo yippee-yay, who is this now coming out of LA?

Snoop Doggy Dogg, produced by Dr. Dre, moving the crowd every single day.

Snoop's smooth Cali flow and his smoky hip-hop haze masked a razor-sharp wit and a biting turn of phrase.

But no one speaks of wit without the Marshall Mathers name.
The lyrics he would spit were anything but tame.

Slim Shady was to Eminem like Dr. Jekyll was to Hyde.
Some people have in them an evil genius deep inside.
Songs like "My Name Is" and the scary story of "Stan"
made Eminem famous: hip-hop's most wanted man.

One of the biggest stars on the whole west side,
this skinny kid named Tupac—a source of California pride.

Suge
Knight

Dr. Dre

The poster boy for "thug life," he seemed to cultivate drama.
But he showed a sensitive side on his song "Dear Mama."

Back in New York City, change was in the air.
A new crew called Bad Boy, led by an illustrious pair.
The big one was Smalls—The Notorious B.I.G.
The other one was Combs—a.k.a. Puff Daddy.

Puff Daddy

Lil' Kim

They sang "Biggie Biggie Biggie" and anyone could see
just how his words were hypnotizing.

Let's pause for a second. This is a PSA.
A public service announcement, as some people say.

THE WU-TANG CLAN AIN'T NOTHING TO MESS WITH.

A clan from Staten Island
made up of 10 MCs,
they had myriad styles
and were known
as Killa Beez.

Over New York City arose an imposing figure.
Most called him Jay Z, or Hova and sometimes Jigga.

Born in the Marcy projects,
that's down in Bed-Stuy,
he could rap about subjects
completely on the fly.

"Hard Knock Life"
was a breakthrough song;
he was a global celebrity
before very long.

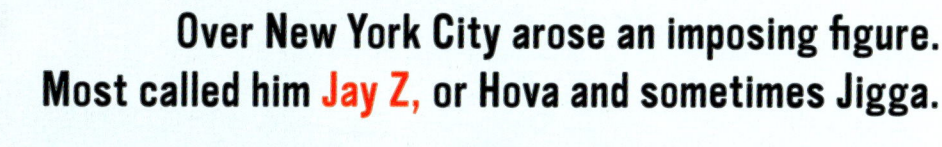

OutKast, down in Atlanta,
call it the "Dirty South,"
had a sweet Southern twang,
and they turned the party out.

In the Virginia
Commonwealth,
another star flies high.
That's where
Missy Elliott
is supa dupa fly.

Chicago's in the Midwest
of the grand old USA.
Some people know it best
as the hometown of Kanye.
We could write a whole book
on our friend Mr. West;
no matter where you look,
he crowns himself the best.

Now let's talk about Nicki—
she's got the super bass.
She flows fast and wicked,
and all up in your face.

Here's another MC flirting
with the avant-garde.
His clever wording
made him rap's new star.
He seems quieter,
more thoughtful by far:
a rapper and a writer,
that's Kendrick Lamar.

In the year 2010,
Drake made his debut.
Don't know where you've been
if you missed the rave reviews.
Drake can rap & act & sing—
he's a true triple threat.
His hit song "Hotline Bling"
was as big as it could get.

With Roman and Barbie
and her other alter egos,
her fans are like an army
following wherever she goes.

By now the culture's spread
to every corner of the globe.
Inside every head
is a hip-hop frontal lobe.

Break-dancing lives on,
they teach graffiti in schools.
MCs have fashion lines,
DJs epitomize cool.

But hip-hop remains, deep down at its heart,
a unique expression, an urban form of art.

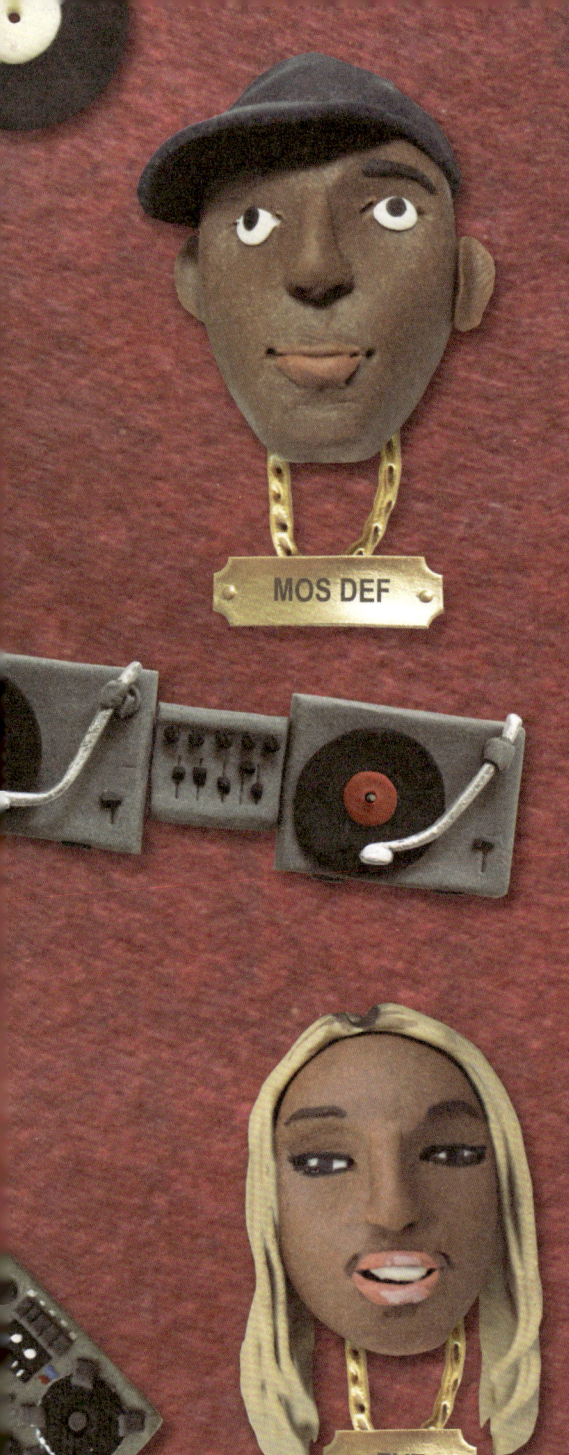

MOS DEF

KOOL DJ RED ALERT

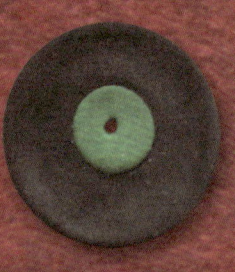

EVE

SLICK RICK